CONTENTS

CHAPTER ONE
LIAM'S WEEKEND . . . 4

CHAPTER TWO
BEING BORED . . . 8

CHAPTER THREE
HELPING OTHERS . . . 18

WHO IS BORED? . . . 22
GLOSSARY . . . 23
TO LEARN MORE . . . 24
INDEX . . . 24

Chapter One

LIAM'S WEEKEND

Liam woke up Saturday morning. It was raining. He could not go outside to play. He wanted something to do.

BORED

by Meg Gaertner

Published by The Child's World®
1980 Lookout Drive • Mankato, MN 56003-1705
800-599-READ • www.childsworld.com

Photographs ©: Shutterstock Images, cover (face and hand), cover (eyes), 1 (face and hand), 1 (eyes), 5, 6, 17, 19; Jingjits Photography/Shutterstock Images, 9; Maria Symchych/Shutterstock Images, 10; LightField Studios/Shutterstock Images, 13; India Picture/Shutterstock Images, 14; iStockphoto, 20, 22 (top left), 22 (top right); Hugh Stonelan/iStockphoto, 22 (bottom left); Valua Vitaly/iStockphoto, 22 (bottom right)

Design Elements: Shutterstock Images

Copyright © 2019 by The Child's World®
All rights reserved. No part of this book may be reproduced or utilized in any form or by any means without written permission from the publisher.

ISBN Hardcover: 9781503828049
ISBN Paperback: 9781622434640
LCCN: 2018944226

Printed in the United States of America
PA02395

ABOUT THE AUTHOR

Meg Gaertner is a children's book author and editor who lives in Minnesota. When not writing, she enjoys dancing and spending time outdoors.

His mom was at work. His sister had homework. His dad was busy with chores. Liam was bored.
He felt there was nothing to do.

Chapter Two
BEING BORED

Sometimes people have a lot of energy. They want to do something. But nothing seems interesting enough. They feel bored.

You might get **distracted** easily. You may even feel as if there is nothing to do. Everyone feels bored sometimes.

It can help to find something to **focus** on. You can be creative. Make up a game. Write a story. Paint a picture.

It can also help to tell others how you feel.
They might have ideas for things you could do.

It is okay to be bored. The feeling will not last forever. You will find something to be interested in.

THINK ABOUT IT
Can you think of a time when you were bored?

Chapter Three

HELPING OTHERS

You can help others who are bored. You can create a fun game. You can **suggest** different activities.

People who are bored might seem distracted or uninterested. That is okay. You can still include them. You can still be their friend.

WHO IS BORED?

Can you tell who is bored? Turn to page 24 for the answer.

GLOSSARY

distracted (diss-TRAKT-ed) To be distracted is to be unable to focus. When you are distracted, your mind jumps from idea to idea.

focus (FOH-kuss) To focus is to think about something or someone. When you focus on something, you give your mind something to do.

suggest (sug-JEST) To suggest something is to put it forward as an idea. A friend may suggest different activities to help when you feel bored.

TO LEARN MORE

Gaertner, Meg. *Disappointed*. Mankato, MN: The Child's World, 2019.

Kreul, Holde. *My Feelings and Me*. New York, NY: Skyhorse Publishing, 2018.

Moore-Mallinos, Jennifer. *A Whole Bunch of Feelings*. Hauppauge, NY: Barron's Educational Series, 2018.

Visit our Web site for links about being bored:
childsworld.com/links

Note to Parents, Teachers, and Librarians: We routinely verify our Web links to make sure they are safe and active sites. So encourage your readers to check them out!

INDEX

chores, 7

games, 12, 18

rain, 4

friend, 21

homework, 7

sister, 7